PRAISE

At first, the poems in *Turkey Vulture* seem like a portal to another place and time—a small town, a lifetime ago. As Heraclitus asserts in one of the book's epigraphs, "No man ever steps in the same river twice, / for it's not the same river / and he's not the same man." Yet in this beautiful collection Zachary Lundgren reminds us that there's no veil between the past and the present. We'll never escape where we came from—the "wrinkled barbwire," the "cow grass and cotton"—but we shouldn't want to. Lundgren doesn't romanticize the past, but he understands its significance: "The river, it's always there. This poem / only turns with time." It's a paradox. In one sense we aren't who we were in our youth. In another, we absolutely are. We are every version of ourselves we've ever been and ever will be.

—Melissa Fite Johnson, 2023 Birdy Poetry Prize Judge, author of *Green*

A modern bucolic collection, Lundgren's poems cut to the heart like an emo song that makes us fall in love with the world we tear down with each coming of age. *Turkey Vulture* is a dazzling debut that leaves us homesick for every version of ourselves.

—Gloria Muñoz, author of *Danzirly*

Turkey Vulture is a meeting of the gothic and the pastoral. Keeping an eye turned to nature, the poems are aware of the vivacity of life and the peculiar experience of facing death.

Love supersedes other aspects of nature, offering such images as, "She steps down the muddy jaw of the river // wanting my hand, so I give it to her. // I give it to her and not even riverwater / is as soft" ("River Luck").

Love extends into what feels like and what doesn't feel like home, as explored in the first poem of each section. Sometimes, all we need to feel like we're at home is someone who "whispers against my sunburned / neck and laughs because this is anything but permanence yet it will never go away" ("Home," section 2). Memories make temporary things permanent to us for as long as we can hold on.

Collectively, these poems are lessons on how once things are gone, they're gone, except in how we savor their memory and their effect on us.

—Linzi Garcia, author of *Thank You*

TURKEY VULTURE

Winner of The Birdy Poetry Prize—2023
by Meadowlark Press

TURKEY VULTURE

Zachary Lundgren

Meadowlark
PRESS
Emporia, Kansas, USA

Meadowlark Press, LLC
meadowlarkbookstore.com
P.O. Box 333, Emporia, KS 66801

Turkey Vulture

Cover photo by Bruce Lundgren

Cover design by TMS, Meadowlark Press

Author photo by Bruce Lundgren

Interior design by Linzi Garcia, Meadowlark Press

POETRY / American / General
POETRY / Subjects & Themes / Nature
POETRY / Subjects & Themes / Family
POETRY / Subjects & Themes / Death, Grief, Loss

ISBN: 978-1-956578-44-7
Library of Congress Control Number: 2023943501

For my family, my parents who always believed in my writing, and Jay Hopler, who revealed the serious and wonderful joy of this craft.

TABLE OF CONTENTS

1

2

3

No man ever steps in the same river twice,
for it's not the same river
and he's not the same man

—Heraclitus

You can't step into the same
river even once,
and why would you want to? You can't

—James Galvin

1

We look at the world once, in childhood.
The rest is memory

—Louise Glück

HOME

There's deerblood dripping on a concrete floor in Lawson's
    barn from the mother deer I killed
with my sister's car so we hung her up in the barn from the
    gambrel roof on the first night
of summer to save her we dressed her right there and cut from
    pelvic to breastbone down
and something fell to the concrete floor a heart I thought but
    no a fetus fell to the concrete
and I saw that I had killed not one but two that summer night
    and I wonder which is worse
taking both mother and child or leaving just one to that night
the first of the summer

YOUTH

Near the church there is a winter cornfield
and a fox
caught in the wire-fence
gnawing at its own leg; a slight bonfire.

God. I wanted to walk but sat down
beneath that aching oak
losing its mind in green and those all-quiet
little flowers.

I did it. That's what she said when she called
and her voice, bare feet
beneath gravel, like-running. I wonder if he
would've had my mouth

CUT

I took my little brother out one night. He wanted to tip cows
because his friends told him cows sleep
standing up and he just couldn't
believe it. We walked through woods out to the Sedlin's
but you don't know them.
After the trees, I held the barbwire fence
for him. The fields were flat and quiet
but a light ahead, a grounded star—it looked
angry. When we found the cows,
I got so pissed because here we were
and now he wouldn't.

But remember: back at the wirefence he didn't
wait and his arm got caught and after
he stood back up he showed me the blood
with a smile the peeled skin and black dripping
because it was night and his whole face smiling
just smiling just smiling just

BLOOD BROTHERS

—after Frank Stanford

Lawson, he lives near the graveyard he can shoot a fat tick off
    a skinny dog and he'll find it
he'll show you.

Sean Austin, he talks with metal and hands a Skoal can in his
    backpocket the halo of some
unimportant angel.

Keeno, he's got cannonball eyes makes the next town over
    white-flag he teaches all the girls
how to sing.

J.O., he's quiet and knows about a garden he sculpts dog heads
    out of clay with his wrists gray
the loudest of us all.

I don't do much but listen to the river and marry myself up in
    a tree the story of how we grow old
then cut to a stump

MORMON GIRLS

Hannah, she never knew the boy who died on black ice last
    February.
Three days later, she's kneeling like a community

center by the road—her altogether hair, black
and quiet and hands green and white with chickweed.

Jill, she danced with me in the carpeted church. She took off
the purple cardigan and I saw her pale shoulders

scratched red after her mother caught her
about to leave the house like that.

Whitney, she sat in the middle of her family in the second pew
each Sunday, still wearing that white dress from the night

before. I couldn't see her face, scratched with whiskey—God
do I love her.

What is in these small towns that makes these girls grow
with such grace? Sing away a Sunday

only to rinse out those kisses with barbwire
scraping soft gums, those no-longer-baby teeth.

Whitney, she wouldn't sleep with me, but listened
the night I told her what it was like. The next morning

I heard her footsteps and she sat there in my bed
God—we laughed like sunlight, we laughed like children

waking up

BRANDED

He was drunk. I'm sure that helped when I took
the cattle iron from the stove like some old red star.

It looked like a relic, I thought, one from some religion
we forgot to read about but lucky we're blood

because blood remembers. I didn't ask if he was
ready because that's how it goes.

The cattle iron bit into his calf and we cheered.
    We were all greedy. That red star sang

in its strange language. After, he laughed, he displayed
his leg like a king like a city-limit sign.

The next summer I collected photographs and red birds
into a bantam fire. I made goodbye

CADDY SMELLED LIKE TREES

We used to play in the creek its snake

tack not the

way a snake moves but the way cotton

mouths hang the trees ones

we

climbed looking for God but

not really just showing we could we won't

pile up like chicken bones in the

corner of a cabin so

off far in the woods people forget

it is there

and it is I smell the little marrow

even taste

it could would dig my hands into

the smoke I will not let

laughter turn all that we have done into perfume her mask

a new life to

shoulder like sick blankets dumb

pretty smiled face I'm left

so at dusk I wander in

to the woods behind our house the big

I walk right into a big oak

and stick my face into its hold but it's November the

tree is quiet

in my nose

DECEMBERISM

Dinner at the only restaurant in town,
we watched one another

like thieves   /   a hand over your chest.

On your birthday, we engraved our names
into your bedsheets; freckles
blossom, then rusting when we fall asleep

on the floor   /   your hair in wildfire across my chest.

Walking home that night, you took
my wrists for examination

a story told short   /   sleepless nights ripen like raspberry
        vines.

You look at me. I still don't know why
there are so many stars

BUGONIA

10th Century, Constantinople

Build a house, ten cubits high, with all the sides of equal
    dimensions, with one door,
and four windows, one on each side; put an ox into it, thirty
    months old, very fat
and fleshy; let a number of young men kill him by beating
    him violently with clubs,
so as to mangle both flesh and bones, but taking care not to
    shed any blood;
let all the orifices, mouth, eyes, nose, etc. be stopped up with
    clean and fine linen,
impregnated with pitch; let a quantity of thyme be strewed
    under the reclining animal,
and then let windows and doors be closed and covered with
    a thick coating of clay
to prevent the access of air or wind. After three weeks have
    passed, let the house be opened,
and let light and fresh air get access to it, except from the
    side from which the wind
blows strongest. Eleven days afterwards, you will find the
    house full of bees,
hanging together in clusters, and nothing left of the ox but
    horns, bones, and hair

21st Century, Loudoun County

Walk out of the house, the one on Lovettsville Road, with
    unwritten hay left in the fields,
with three doors and ten windows, with an old Volkswagen;

walk outside, two-hundred
and thirty months old; there is a girl waiting for you in the
    mouth of the gravel driveway,
dusted in warpaint and a skinny smile, waiting to kill you.
    She will not shed any blood;
let your mouth, eyes, nose, etc. be earthed with the soft silk
    of nostalgia,
impregnated with music, old; let her examine your stitches
    like a guiltless doctor,
let her pretend she does not know how to handle weapons;
    like when she would
kiss your neck and let light and fresh air get access to it. You
    think that eleven days
afterwards, she will blossom for you again like a house full
    of bees, hanging together
with pretty eyes and honey. When you speak, a bluebird
    arcs, falls
buckshot to your no-winged tomorrow, that which you both
    share

THE BACKBONE BEFORE BLOSSOM

—after Sally Mann's "Candy Cigarette"

Daughters in this town, they fly for city-limit signs
unripe footsteps color bridges

they kill cardinals. But after the weekend, after every
weekend, she's back at the McDonald's across

from the high school, thinking about strawberry
but orders the chocolate milkshake.

Daughters in this town, they stick like dandelion-heads
patchworked through wrinkled barbwire.

Entangled up in cow grass and cotton, they star
against dusk in a sky no one

is watching. Her white dress, it's not a flag, but
a promise: summer grass will eventually rot in your mouth.

Daughters in this town, they break curfews and dress codes,
hearts and a long Sunday fast. They are broken

and are the breakers. She knows this with a fist before Christianity
hurt, before there was such a thing as memory

A CONVERSATION BETWEEN ROADKILL
AND THE BOY

"Is this as good as it gets?"

> "For us?" the boy asked.

"Us."

> "I don't think so."

"How does it get any better? After this."

> "Well, we all grow up, get jobs, get married."

"We?"

> "Sorry."

"It's okay. That doesn't sound all that great anyway."

> "No?"

"What's the point if you can already see all the way down the road?"

> "That's funny."

"Don't you know how the movie ends?"

> "Well—"

"You know how it ends."

"Like this. Like you."

"So why sit down and watch? Why drive that road?"

"Because trees and the ocean—I think sex makes you happy, for a little while."

"I wish this gravel was as soft as you"

THE HARDNESS OF A GIRL DRINKING
BEER // THE SOFTNESS OF BLOOD IN
MY MOUTH

I hear him first, the Mormon kid vomiting
out the back of his pickup
shaking like a boy on a first date and

clean somehow his shirt white
we all laugh
someone hands him another beer

and a soldier shows up at the barn all mean
with a head-cut and the girl I love
he shouts loud and he laughs like a man

who doesn't believe in God talks
to God hardly even tries and has me spitting out secrets
pieces of teeth thin white splinters

taste like milk the girl I love says she can't kiss me
with my busted lip
against the barn slats we are

and we are loud with the soldier finally deserted
she's drunk I'm not
telling her the way she flints against me the way my chest

vices at her voice we sleep
alone
back at the pickup I ask him I don't know why

because he can hardly press out a moan

his white shirt just goes grinning in the dark
how many I ask does it take to really forget

he asks me for another
but the night sky is a secret
we all told already

I sit away from the barn the voices
the light grazes my split lip my cut tongue a finger coated in
    dirt
that becomes soil and I know that all this is rain or the smell
    just before

A HYPOTHESIS ON WHY WE ONLY FUCK IN GRAVEYARDS WHEN WE'RE YOUNG

Tonight, all of America seems to love us
because we'll never
die. I open a bag of peanuts with one hand
and we talk like we know

the headstones. My father's church is made of dirt
and trees. We walk through the dark
like crossing into West Virginia
for a strip club in the woods—neon signs

colored dangerous as snakes. When we sit in the grass
she shows me her hands and tells me
she believes there was altruism
even before we had God.

Chapstick falls out of her pocket and she can't tell the difference
between Virginia and pitch pine
in this dark and does it
matter? We make stories

about the stone-names around us and under us and how
the trees are so incredibly primary. My head
is breaking open through my mouth and I hope
it's like candy

to her. She pulls her ankles out of the grass and peanuts
scatter like gunshot birds. In quiet
she takes off her pants and
I hear a whistle.
I do not look because fear
made him look back before leaving the underworld, before this

YOU ARE WORTH MORE THAN
MANY SPARROWS

and the whitetail,
doctored into venison, smoking by the oaks
out back into black air because who doesn't
have a soul?

You are worth more than water,
than empires of roots
braiding cold dirt, twisting up trees
like a language that isn't dead
quite yet.

You beautify the forest with a gaze,
a center. You are the jar
on top of a Tennessee hill
filled with fire, with plastic.

You and I, we know we are worth more than an acre
of old growth, a river of salmon,
a small pair of sparrows. If not,

then why do we not only pray to but actually believe
in this strip-mall god's flirting smile
capricious as gas prices off highways reaching they keep reaching
and do we ever arrive?

THE RADIO HELPS ME BELIEVE IN FATE

Driving home, tired and god-eyed, you tell me
a song is proof we live in circles.
An old t-shirt can be home
on nights now warm, not dark.

A song is proof we live in circles
says a girl who does not love me
on nights now warm, not dark
like summer grass and the grass is sharp.

A girl who does not love me
looks at me like the third of July, like a rope untied
in summer grass, the grass is sharp.
When she laughs, it's just cursive in my head

on the third of July, a rope untied,
looking like a handful of chickweed.
Her smile goes cursive in my head
and looks nothing like a promise.

Like a handful of chickweed
we grew up here, remember.
Our hands look nothing like a promise.
This song is proof we live in circles

just circling each other, everything that is remembered.
I forgot the windshield wipers. I forgot
how this song is proof we live in circles
and how love is as simple as standing out in the rain.
I forgot the windshield wipers

as the rain breaks on us, and somehow,
home is as simple as standing out in the rain.
One morning, out collecting chickweed, you told me:

the rain will break on us, and somehow,
our hands. After this, you will know where to belong
in the morning, collecting chickweed, you ask me
tired, all god-eyed: can we go home?

A DEAD DEER ON THE SIDE OF THE ROAD WITH A "GET WELL SOON" BALLOON TIED TO ITS LEG

We buried Johnny on Christmas
eve. I sat in the front pew, cotton
mouthed and a new haircut. I watched his father sit straight
    as a lie.

The taste of prayer against my tongue, just a wooden sword.
Oh, the black knight
rides again

2

The buzzard stops
and becomes a star

—Tomas Tranströmer

HOME

There's herblood on her thigh and mine and Sunday
    morning is open mouth and drooling
with sunlight slipping through basement windows making
    blonde our skin in the after
after we pretend to carve a bed out of blankets she whispers
    against my sunburned
neck and laughs because this is anything but permanence
    yet it will never go away
and dusk answers like it knows better quiet children and
    she combs my hair and I kiss
the constellation of acne along her cheek this making will
    let us stop thinking for just
a moment about the old barn they tore down across town
    to put up a second
grocery store I kiss her teeth and she makes me remember
    what is stolen and how
we can one day get it back

FIRST LOVE

After stuffing the dead starling into a coke bottle,
I cast the glass downriver
and opened the cut
down my finger that always looks like you

RIVER LUCK

Love and a cough cannot be concealed.
Even a small cough. Even a small love
—Anne Sexton

Don't think baptism: this is before
        all that. She said she wants to keep

        her hair dry. She steps down and oh—
this must be what spring does to trees.

She steps down the muddy jaw of the river
        wanting my hand, so I give it to her.

        I give it to her and not even riverwater
is as soft. What reasons does this river even have for us?

The riverwater takes her hips, her breasts, small shoulders
        they laugh carelessly in the sun.

        Even though we talk like children,
there's a hint of distance in your face, the good kind,

like knowing. The river, it's always there. This poem
        only turns with time. There is

        no conflict here but time.
It's the same as why our bones refuse to rot away

THE SUMMER WAR

This town has two grocery stores now
and only one graveyard
I spread a map across the dashboard and slit
a catfish open to find my father
and end up running back to my wrists such sweet guarantee
it's no different than the day I was born
to look up and see the girls go practically glowing
off of late July the suggestion
cigarette pockets a radio song asking bones to
shake just a little so I shake
and climb tall trees and dig up river dirt
just to sit on an empty flatbed truck in hopes to outlast all
    these metaphors
it doesn't make us selfish just because every war
begins with a question so I ask
the oak leaves of their green exile I ask
the catfish but he is unclever I ask
the all-knowing mud and lose patience

I believe one evening with just enough salt
I won't have to die
I will unriddle this pulse this tale is just the warming shiver
    of green cicadas

THE GOAT FLOWERS

Stop complaining about the old barn they tore down for
     another grocery store.

Boys fly across the world to die and I go the next town over
     to ask a stone lion serious questions.

Streets here tend to be named after southern generals and
     one is a river.

I want to kiss her even with that little childhood left in her
     cheeks.

The story is we are only allowed to live once without a
     seatbelt.

J.O. said he saw a mountain lion in town but I thought we
     called them cougars.

You told me twice how your sister broke her wrist for love at
     the water tower.

Cowboy Bob loves his wife and chews tobacco so tell me
     again how to live.

When was it we stopped believing flowers their numbered
     petals telling us who to love?

THIRTEEN

Sister,

Do you remember that first home, the big white one
with gothic windows and the spiral staircase
descending down into a dark confederate basement?

Do you remember walking to the corner
store and stuffing our pockets with candy
bought with dollars made out of cut grass?

Do you still run to collect fireflies and ladybugs
in jars made soft with the same grass?
I think about my legs all the time, now.

Sister,

Do you remember when we moved that spring
to a quarter-acre lot across town?
We gutted that old house of us: tables and chairs, action

figures and blue pillows. A mason jar with grass.
I held the jar to my face and there was twilight
and tootsie rolls and fireflies mapping out

a summer. I opened the jar and found four black husks.
Shaking it even, I couldn't find
any ladybugs

THE FIELDS CHASE YOU WHEN NO ONE ELSE WILL

January

After a dance, I drove her home and it wasn't much
of a mattress that pin oak
but into the ground, and then it was over. I kissed her hair.

February

I talk to the morning as it numbs the fingertips of trees.
Grass favors its roots, crowning brown
then yellow, and tired.
But these sleeping fields are not asleep
they often sing
early in little light before the deer.
I heard this once (but not in her voice)
and we are still left fallow.

March

There are seeds in the wind I turn and
in my mouth.
I have not seen her in months but the fields
have and this might be why
out of the ground the heart, its homecoming
raw and emerald, always chasing
always just about to catch

IT'S RAINING OUTSIDE AND WE WON'T LIVE FOREVER

That night we forgot we were in love, starlight
got stuck up in the sky. I turn over to write the time
on the clock on my hand. I don't

know why. Hair and sheets tangling like some strategy. I ask
if you saw the blue on the bluebirds—is that
what makes them bluebirds?

You don't know what time it is. You slide a bracelet
down your arm and say I wasn't
really looking

HEARTLAND

Too poor to even think about stealing Jack, the boys grab
    Old Crow
and run for the goat bridge
because one day they might actually

make it. But legs and hearts, they can fail—caught up in the
    quicksand
of simple economics. Fishing
without any bait, we're always here.

Too poor to even bother stealing the boys, the girls work
    quick
scribbling down burgers and milkshakes
for ghosts not quite dead. The worst

kind of ghosts. But it's the only DQ for forty miles and
    there's that
ketchup smile. In a killed truck, she cleans
the dirt from her Easter nails.

They stand together in the dirt and watch a pickup truck
    coming
out of the cornfield with a doe
in the back. Good dirt

and first blood but they don't even see how her eyes look
    just
like theirs going nowhere into town
we were always taught to run

RULE 1: ALL SWINE MUST BE EAR NOTCHED

This tree I am hanging from is an oak
but I cannot tell
what kind

RULE 2: ONLY WOOD CHIPS WILL BE ALLOWED FOR BEDDING

Where is home? I read of a tribe that once thrived
on these high plains. Their men were named only

after their first scars. But what do I know of blood, of
hunger? I stroke her long hair into sadness, because

of it. Our traditions look different, but they remain
the same. The year after my first buck,

I climbed her barbwire fence and it complained
it broke red into my arm, a prayer pretending.

But that scar, it doesn't speak here. Or maybe no one is
listening or I'm translating it all wrong

RULE 3: ALL SWINE, INCLUDING THE CHAMPIONS, MUST BE SLAUGHTERED

At the Story County Fair, I fell in love with a girl
blonde and sweet
as the cornfields and

      just as necessary.

This wasn't home. I doubt she could see the dog
wood bloom-talking from
my chest

      but it was—it was aching, no—descanting the Iowa air.

Like this county, the fairgrounds are small and polite
and then it's not. I watched his hand
slide down the front of her

      unbuttoning her jeans, unbuttoning his hog-smile.

The smell of barbecue and cotton candy
compelled this flavored disgust
from my throat. Kneeling behind some thrill ride, breathing.

      My mouth: a hole that nothing will fill.

It wasn't close to harvest so when I ran
into the fields and stripped away an ear
the taste was just too sweet

RULE 4: THE JUDGE HAS THE AUTHORIZATION TO DISQUALIFY ANY PIGS THAT ARE SEVERELY UNSOUND

1

Here, the oaks grow imperial as kings
in exile. Telephone poles bridge better
than anything from my mouth. I tell
myself: climbing a tree, digging a hole is not looking
for God.

I will be judged in front of the oak.

2

Why do we look to the sky when the fields
instruct us, every six months, this trick of
resurrection? They know the secret.
They know the answer over and over
and over us they brag with gold mouthfuls of green.

I will be judged by the river who took two children
last spring.

3

I still taste her shoulders, sun-
peeled, a little summer left in my mouth
and like a blackberry seed she is the center.
Looking is just an excuse. She walks towards me in a white dress
and I am the one who cannot stop bleeding.

I will be judged, here, by the spell and the length
of my silence

RULE 5: ONCE YOUR TRAILER ENTERS THE FAIR GROUNDS, SWINE, UNLOADED OR NOT, WILL NOT BE ALLOWED TO RETURN HOME

Summer is dead. Stop trying to talk to it. Take down
that red sky so we can stack up
the bed of this diesel truck; humming, anxious to cross
the state line. Let's go.

I was warned. They say that the prairie air can starch
your words until even the corn won't listen.
Maybe that's why we didn't speak that day, the last
one. Instead, we traced maps

along each other's arms, the muscles and veins,
freckles to remember. We sat there in a field
of soy. There was a time for her mouth
and then there wasn't.

The way her dress crossed over her knees made me think
of wood-smoke, a goldfinch
drunk with flight. That's when she took
a prairie rose and she planted it

behind my ear with a limping smile because she knew
it would not stay. But we know. We know that just
because the flower wouldn't stay
doesn't mean it isn't still there

THE GRASS IN YOUR HAIR

You look almost dead, lying there in that summer field
if not for your little foxing smile.

I would wake you. I would tell you where the blackberries
almost cry to be found, to bless us

because we speak the same. Your smile in song: *Life really ain't
    all that tragic*

TO MISSPELL THE NAME "CRUSH"

It has never rained in this town on the Fourth of July and just

the other day a boy tried to drown himself

in Lincoln Creek. I heard this theory that we are all

connected, and yet, we live apart. Maybe that's why
    Schopenhauer gutted love

because he could not have it. When I find you on a hill, hair
    clinging your face

like a child's name handwritten, I do not remember any frogs
    falling

from the sky. I do remember the carousel in my head of dusk

and summer and basement couches. We are

that age: still expecting love stories to have a teleological bent.

We are that age: we know nothing yet of stories

made by decision. I find you on a hill

in the rain and I find your cheekbone with my mouth. The rain
    doesn't

stop (in the stories

it stops). And we rot at this—this goodbye, and this

rained-hill may be the last place I ever find you

again. But now I don't remember the words I brought to say.

I try to speak like my father and chew on the words

and they taste all wrong. Copper, bones. I would break

you but you look at me, up at me, and the rain

quiets. Children emerge from cars to set off firecrackers

and they pop, they fight.

A few people clap as the fireworks make a holiday

in the parking lot. You tell me the end of summer makes
you

glad because you saw it. In the rain, and then not in the
rain,

our decision to be sad doesn't matter. I know I cannot

look back. I look

back. I hold my wrist tightly, very tight

3

I didn't mean I'd seen everything, John Grady said.
I know you didn't.
I just meant I'd seen some things I'd as soon not of.
I know it. There's hard lessons in this world.
What's the hardest?
I don't know. Maybe it's just that when things are gone
   they're gone. They ain't comin' back

—Cormac McCarthy

HOME

There's myblood on my shirt from the football game we lost to
    County again but even after
a friend touched my mouth a Friday night walking home
    beneath October and a cotton moon
crossing the water tower the one I never tried to climb but
    talked about climbing
an old woman who owned horses in the hills told me when one
    died or delivered stillborn
she'd drive up the gulley some miles the tires on her truck low
    with the weight of dead
things and the cougars waited on the rocks this agreement like
    the one we make every
day but it's so quiet we often forget about gravity or the machine
    of words in my head
or how in the dark it's hard to see poison ivy no there is a
    softness in my chest revealing
itself in quiet and clever ways maybe one day maybe it could be
    full it could be a religion
strong as dirt and maybe it's here

WE WERE NEITHER SMALL NOR GREAT
BUT GROWING

When you were seventeen, I touched your thigh
and felt your heart.
It's an itch, Sunday morning this gravel road
after church. The radio has a few good ideas
and your smile swells. We could go out there and lay our hands
down in the grass like dogwood
leaves like a lost pair of shoes.

If it wasn't for the book in your backseat
we would've died together that day
a little, the little scar along your cheek
the rabbit along the split-rail fence
now here in my chest. They say it's always this way
when we dogwoods
grow close—but not

AGONY AND MEAT, EVERYTHING PLAIN AFTERWARDS

The morning after her funeral, I watched day
light thicken with early air
like blood clotting my throat.

Now, each day will be long. The sun will come, repose
and go rusting on these lips and tongue.
My father built this front porch the year before.

And here I am, talking like a tree
stump with that hornet hive we avoided all summer
now without the hive

JUST DRINK THE WATER

1

River, keep quiet. She locks the door to my truck and then I
    cannot

breathe. The kudzu keeps
creeping for my chest.

I don't know her middle name but can taste that coffin
    beneath her ear

all gold tangled hair
it's sweeter, it's here.

2

River, come follow. Maybe it's the beer making the bed of
    this pickup so soft.

Maybe it's her
daisy way of looking over

those fields. A sign says this was a Civil War battleground,
    but history doesn't

matter right now.
The stars, they forget.

3

River, go blossom like hair in her mouth as we climb around one
    another reckless
like bittersweet my hands now they pray to that god the red one
who lives for only a few minutes and thankful
we should be for these prayers
that are just prayers

HARPERS FERRY

I wanted to write a poem about trying to swim
across the Potomac river
and failing. I wanted to compare this
to John Brown's raid, to Robert E. Lee's rifle.
I wanted to marry these failures, these rebellions
of guns and legs, and wring
a little victory out of loss
like a horse collapsing simply because
he's outrun his lungs.
I couldn't. I can't. Mountains or molehills, an angel
is more than a handshake.
Lying on wet rocks, I try to recapture each breath,
my lungs retelling this broken story,
relearning this lesson. All the while,
the river is bored into silence

NAILS

She hammers at an old stump all Christmas'd with nails
in dusky field-light off a bonfire. She misses. She laughs

like how blonde hair plays in daylight;
there's an infancy to this language. He walks over

and gathers her small shoulders like a stranger collecting
    firewood
from your backporch. Your hands, they itch

at this. The firelight waits, is sad. You go and piss
your philosophy into the grass—the only one

listening because no one is drinking
what they need. Water is just not strong enough

to wash that first nail out of your mouth. No one knows
love until it's hammered through their cheeks

CHILD OF GOD

Bobby, he was fat as shit. He wore glasses like those kids
in old movies, crooked and thick, like a witch's curse

right on his face. In gym class, the boys traded days laughing
at him or feeling sorry, but never both

at the same time. I'm sure he was poor. Is that why
he loved NASCAR, the Stars and Bars,

and dirty jokes he'd say out in the open
to anyone (right to your face

like those glasses)? After high school, I heard
his father died. Does it matter how?

Like the beautiful girls who don't look back at you, God
hates us all

just a little. But that doesn't explain any of this

YOU DON'T NAME DEAD THINGS

1
I think about my bones too often these days.
I walk behind a girl in those boots.
I taste that early itch of air, that bit of sugar
I chew on this and would sing,
but come on.

2
She wears a white dress in the fields.
She does not surrender to the walk.
She finds the horse half-covered in bluegrass
she kneels to it with closed eyes
two seeds in winter.

3
We arrived late to the decay, the horse's gut made cave.
We taste a tightness in our throats, this.
We close our eyes, but wait—wait
she says,
I wait to begin digging

HAPPY BOY

I changed a water filter for my father today
I saw a red-tailed hawk.

After, I made a killer soup and shared
dinner with Zane and J.O.

we talked about clocks, about metaphors.
We understood gold but nothing like forgetting.

It is incredibly important, Zane told me,
to remember how each one of us

is going to heaven; how each of us saw
that red-tailed hawk

AN HOUR BEFORE TURKEY VULTURES CLOT THE SKY

Out of mud and mulberry, the fox blazed like a prophecy
made real, splitting chicory and clover
the dry face of the road kicked to a cloud.

Blue took after it like a shadow made quiet
under a loud sun.
A bright July morning already sweating with plans.

The fox had the dirt road but never
a chance. Young
and hungry-skinny, I saw when Blue pinned it

and bit into its neck—the sound deep as bone, as
a secret, as a lost ritual
found.

After, in the tall grass, I stroked Blue's fur and it wasn't blood
coating him. It was the morning
dew on my hands

A MEMORY THAT IS MORE LIKE AN ELEGY

It's summer and the grass is new like the way girls dress, bright
and dangerous as Disneyland.

My father and I drive out looking for a fishing hole he knows
is gone.

On the road, we have already seen three Starbucks.
Three.

We watch the hills sweeten into wine as these stories get
more expensive.

My father tells me the only birds he ever sees out here now
are vultures

HYPERBOLE

Hyperbole says more than reality warrants, yet what is true
is understood from the false, as he could split the very rocks
by his eloquence, to touch the sky with his finger

—Erasmus

When I tell you that your eyes are stars, it is
because collagen fibers occasionally catch dead light.

When I say that your laughter is a song, I am referencing
2,000 hertz, one octave above a soprano's high C.

When I sigh that my heart beats for you, I am just
confusing you with oxygen.

And when I confess that I miss you
I am just hungry, again.

But that morning, the one I told you I would die
for almost nothing but you, it wasn't a lie—
       early Sunday scriptures reading to
       your family and tears talking through
       my eyes, does this mean I believe?

WHEN I WAS SLEEPING, THEY TALKED TO ME, THEY'D GO IN MY DREAMS

The wheat fields over everything.
Our hands, and.

Down in them I felt like drowning,
but a dry air
paved this road in my mouth,

soft. The fields of young gold shaking
like our voices, so all you had
to do was shout
and I'd run

like fire
catching across wheat and wheat
to your arms, they.

You died later in a river. The wheat fields never away,
we become erosion: what's left

                                after the sun sheds its gold,
                                opening our just-born eyes

JUSTICE

The blind horse was so old we had to water down his oats.
    My hair
grew long that summer and June, she'll speak to you, but
don't forget she's a liar—spinning all this into something jeweled
when really it's just dirt beneath my nails,
gas in my brother's car. I hook the bucket of oats to the fence
and wait for him. Mosquitos
already. This is a type of love. Who gets to decide what is fable
and what isn't? I lost faith
in the softer afternoon, stroking the horse's flank while he ate
from the bucket. He had another summer
maybe. Out in that field, I told him that when I die
I want all my family and those I could never love
to take me to a river and spread lunch
over my coffin: bread, cheese, enough whiskey.
The river will keep. I stroke the horse and feel dusk
even with that sun.
What is the word for firewood thrown into a fire
right before it burns?
It took me that whole summer to understand that horse's name

WASHED UP ON THE BANKS OF
THE SHENANDOAH

fishing line tangled into knots still knotting

a boot the color of young buffalo, naked silly without laces

half a Faulkner novel, the one with the bloody corncob

    you must be here

snakeskin this thin it's mostly sunlight

a plastic grocery bag jellyfishing

green bra from a late-summer girl, it must

    but wait—beneath mud, beneath the mud

coke cans because this country is a promise

bluegill bones

glass broken to star in a dirty sky

    my mouth my eyes—oh there, that young blood-
        pumper, now home in the method of a dead bird

'SBLOOD

John the Apostle wrote that Jesus   wept;

Cormac McCarthy, that the bird   flew.

What else is there

to say?

There is no   god

but the one that makes us like a whetting stone   makes

PUBLICATION ACKNOWLEDGMENTS

I am grateful to the editors of the following publications in which the following poems in this book first appeared:

A Lonely Riot Magazine, "Bugonia"

Barnstorm Journal, "Quietus"

Cleaver Magazine, "Branded"

Clockhouse, "The Backbone Before Blossom"

FLARE, "You Don't Name Dead Things"

Gravel, "Rule 3: All Swine, Including the Champions, Must Be Slaughtered"

The Louisville Review, "The Fields Chase You When No One Else Will"

Squalorly, "Blood Brothers"

The Tishman Review, "Decemberism"

Wisconsin Review, "First Love"

NOTES

"Blood Brothers" is titled after and inspired by a poem by Frank Stanford.

"Caddy Smelled Like Trees" is inspired by William Faulkner's *The Sound and the Fury*, exploring the character Benjy's point of view.

"Bugonia" is a Greek word, coined by Virgil, for the belief that bees were generated from the dead carcass of a cow. The 10th-century portion of the poem comes from *Geoponica*.

"The Backbone Before Blossom" is inspired by Sally Mann's photograph, "Candy Cigarette."

"You Are Worth More Than Many Sparrows" is from the New International Version Bible, Matthew 10:31.

The epigraph in "River Luck" is from Anne Sexton's poem "Small Wire."

The titles of all five "Rule" poems come from the Story County Fair Association Swine Competition Guidelines.

"Agony and Meat, Everything Plain Afterwards" is from the poem "Santa Lucia" by Robert Hass.

The epigraph in "Hyperbole" is from Erasmus, the Dutch Renaissance writer and scholar.

"When I Was Sleeping, They Talked to Me, They'd Go in My Dreams" is inspired by the Terrence Malick film *Days of Heaven*.

ABOUT THE AUTHOR

Zachary Lundgren was born in California and received his MFA in poetry from the University of South Florida. He has been published in several literary magazines and reviews, including *The Columbia Review*, *The Wisconsin Review*, *Clockhouse*, *Beecher's Magazine*, and *The Louisville Review*. He received his PhD in rhetoric and composition from East Carolina University and now resides in Denver, Colorado.

Meadowlark POETRY

Books are a way to explore, connect, and discover. Poetry incites us to observe and think in new ways, bridging our understanding of the world with our artistic need to interact with, shape, and share it with others.

Publishing poetry is our way of saying—

We love these words,
we want to preserve them,
we want to play a role in sharing them
with the world.

Meadowlark Press
— since 2014 —

meadowlarkpoetrypress.com

Follow Meadowlark Press
on Facebook & Instagram

(f) facebook.com/ReadAMeadowlarkBook

(O) @meadowlarkbooks

BIRDY POETRY PRIZE WINNERS

2022
Cupping Our Palms
Jonathan Greenhause

"These provocative, trustworthy poems owe their strength to narrators who are not afraid to confront their own sense of awe, misgivings, and incredulity, as it pertains to their various stations in life. The prevailing subject of parenthood, and what it means to shepherd children through the stages of growth, keeps circling in this superb collection. . ."
–Bart Edelman, *Whistling to Trick the Wind*

2021
Knowing Is a Branching Trail
Alison Hicks

"*Knowing is a Branching Trail* captured my attention. I read in search of moments that create a soft pause in me. Time given back to me that allows me to sit with feeling, safely and freely. There were voices in the work that transitioned from stranger to companion. It felt as if we shared an understanding. . . I felt less alone with this book."
–Huascar Medina, *Un Mango Grows in Kansas*

2020
Selected Poems: 2000-2020
JC Mehta

"With sharp and incisive language, each piece provides an immersive moment, inviting the reader into the experience of growing up half Cherokee, of self-harm and losing friends, of teaching and aging and loving and living in the Pacific Northwest. Nothing is veiled, nothing is alluded to, and their humor is ever-present, wry and witty."
–Brenna Crotty, Editor, *Selected Poems*

2019
A Certain Kind of Forgiveness
Carol Kapaun Ratchenski

"There is a worldliness in these poems, the kind of grit that accompanies a strong heart. There's awareness–of the self, of the world. And the poems are populated with the magical, husky things of this earth: warm beer in Berlin, rice in a bowl in a monastery, and stains from fresh cranberries. These are poems we can savor, now and again."
–Kevin Rabas, *More Than Words*

Meadowlark Press created The Birdy Poetry Prize to celebrate the voices of our era. Cash prize, publication, and 50 copies awarded annually.

Accepting Entries: September 1 - December 1

Entry Fee: $25

Prize: $1,000 cash, publication by Meadowlark Press, 50 copies of the completed book

All entries will be considered for standard Meadowlark publishing contract offers, as well.

Full-length poetry manuscripts (55 page minimum) will be considered. Poems may be previously published in journals and/or anthologies, but not in full-length single-author volumes. Poets are eligible to enter, regardless of publishing history.

See birdypoetryprize.com for complete submission guidelines. Also visit us at meadowlarkbookstore.com.

www.ingramcontent.com/pod-product-compliance
Lightning Source LLC
Chambersburg PA
CBHW060255030426
42335CB00014B/1709